WHERE THE
TIME GOES

WHERE THE TIME GOES

GALE RENEE WALDEN

GusGus Press • Bedazzled Ink Publishing
Fairfield, California

978-1-945805-09-7 paperback

Cover photo
Booky by Patty Carroll from the series Anonymous Women

Cover Design
by

DESIGNS

GusGus Press
a division of
Bedazzled Ink Publishing Company
Fairfield, California
http://www.bedazzledink.com

For Patty Jo, My First Word

Contents

I.

II.

III.

I.

Postcard

My friend: the ocean is waving from me to you.
The breeze blowing the cornfields is direct.
Here the Virgin Mary is in the backyard
hidden by ivy, and every time I try to pray
I think better of it, a godly itch left unscratched.
The porch is in ruin, just the way I like it.
Across the street the waves crash
into a house of glass and the inhabitants pretend
they haven't been hurt. In the street
Drag Queens are undressing in parades
as the sea breeze transforms silk contour to innocence,
whiskey to aftershave, light to paint.
Days go by. I tell each passing person
that the man I love is a book
and I'm open and we're all, after all, being read.
Disclosure is discouraged
so I learn to parade formally,
in linen. I am not hated
because I am not what I appear.
Still in this deep house of summer night
I am always taking a chance with memory.
Last night I dreamed that sirens
floated up and down your street;
I transposed them into foghorns
and all the light houses beckoned
you back. Everything is the same.
I still pursue the distant green light
Settling for salutation. *First, last, and always.*
Remember?

Autobiography

In the dining room the baby
is crawling on the braided rug.
Around and around the table
she goes. This is important
to itself in the telling of the story
of the girl's life, which is important
to the baby only peripherally.

In the archway between the dining room
and the living room, the girl is four.
The mother is in the kitchen
separated from the girl and the baby
by swinging half doors.
In the side den the phonograph
is resolving itself over and over
into a song about heartbreak.

In the kitchen the mother
is her own magician. She
knows how to make things
float in Jell-o, how to transfer
her voice from womb to room
as she calls into the girl
not to let the baby touch wood.

But the girl is already revolving
like a record herself, she is already
grooving herself out into different songs
as she orbits from one doorway to the other,
the baby crawling toward the outer edge
of the rug to touch the girl spinning like a top.

The mother's head and legs appear,
her whole middle a mystery,
"Why can't you do as I say?"
and because that's not enough
to stop the girl,
she declares Buddy Holly dead.

The girl understands that anyone thin
enough to spin inside the record
will be dead. The girl understands
that the pain of the words and the guitar
could kill anyone, but she doesn't understand
the mother's anger which has now
harmonized with words and guitar.

Perhaps the mother sees
the type of magic the girl will come to,
that the girl will choose
what is not there, what
is in the air, floating
without benefit of slow congelation.

But this is later in the story.
Now there was a setting.
The wood in the doorway
was dark. It was summer.
The baby was already problematic:

It was the first time
I remembered music.

Pink Flamingos

They were the lesser-chinned version of the stork—
the kind of bird that liked babies fine,
but didn't want to carry any of their own,
preferring a dry martini with olives.

They owned the lawns like a cocktail hour
for the middle class, the skinny aluminum legs
poked in John Wayne stance into green grass,
inviting Dad home to TV dinners divided
into visible pockets of shiny, shiny foil and custard.

But our moms weren't high-heeled,
pearl-draped, bouffant babes.
They were feminists who weren't sure
they wanted babies but didn't get paid
enough not to have them. Their kitchens
imploded into a fury of orange shag carpet,
and the *I Hate To Cook Book*
sat open on top of avocado stoves.

Only when we were released to school
did the Moms put on shoulder pads
and stomp out of bi-leveled houses,
leaving keys around our necks,
but the final Baby Boomers
were too late to open history.
We were going to miss everything
except *The Brady Bunch*.

We didn't know; we thought
we were going to be part of a revolution;
playing Woodstock in the flower beds,
near aluminum pools, where the adults
had begun dismantling the plastic birds
watching over us, their heads bent bashfully down.

Later, in college, every time
we saw a pink flamingo that had migrated into kitsch
we'd start laughing—a symptom of love.
We winked at them, played pranks with them,
planting them in the middle of the night
like a dream. Like any good joke, we didn't
understand how we could miss something
right in front of us. And here's the truth:
even if we had known about pet rocks
even if we had known about striped bell-bottoms
or disco or streaking; even if we had known
how stupid our youth was going to be,
we still would have seeded ourselves
into this particular camp, bowing
our regrets onto random, spring lawns.

Dead Poets' Houses

I don't know exactly how it came up in the conversation,
But a woman I didn't know, next to a man I didn't know,
Suddenly said, "I love poets' houses, but I hate
How they pin the dresses to the wall."
That comment wasn't any more unusual than anything
Anyone else had said that day and I would have let it go
But the ubiquity of dresses on the walls in poets' houses
Bothered her so much that she repeated her disdain,
Causing me to question how it was that I had never seen
A dress on any of the many walls in any of the many houses
Where at least one person thought a poet lived.
I started to question my powers of observation
And also to consider whether the absence of a dress
On my own walls signified lack of literary ambition,
Or whether an embroidered shawl counted.
I got that far down the wrong road in my mind
Before I thought about a brick sidewalk in Amherst
Leading up to a house in which hung a thin white dress
Of Emily Dickinson's.
I said, "Oh, you mean Dead Poets' Houses,"
And the man said, "There's a title,"
Which is the language I've been speaking in lately.
At least it was a mental malapropism that got caught early,
Not like the ones I've been living with for forty years—
Misplaced ideas that are so ingrained in my habits of thinking
That an opening to correctness only flies by
Every once in a while and doesn't land.
It's easy to see how wrong knowledge begins innocently.
My daughter comes home from kindergarten repeating
What she's learned about the world:
Abraham Lincoln was killed during a puppet show,
There are 50 states in a year,

Jesus says that all children are better
Than all adults, so I should just quit yelling.
And that's just the beginning of how we learn
What we don't know. There's also the educational vacation.
Maybe this woman's parents drove her to poet houses
While mine were stuck on Ulysses S. Grant.
Just to make sure, I said, "Are we only talking
Emily Dickinson?" and the woman said,
"No, those dresses are in every poet's house,"
And that it was the tiny pins fastening the dresses
To the wall which frightened her the most.
It didn't make sense. Would Elizabeth Bishop
Pin up dresses? Are there fashion statements
In that house of Carl Sandburg's I keep passing
In Galesburg? The man I didn't know said he had a friend
Who wrote a poem about Hart Crane's house
And historical societies called him up to chat.
It turned out the Crane house lived only in his mind,
And I thought maybe this was true of the dresses too.
I took a train away from the conversation,
Back to a flooded basement and I would have been
Happy to conjure up any other house to live in
But the mildew interfered with imagination.
A bird flew in the window I had opened
To air out the house,
And I thought of Wallace Stevens with all those
Blackbirds whirling by him in his study.

There's a lot of ways the mind could travel with this:
Me, I've decided to be happy for strangers.

Road Trip

How I came to live in a motel in Pittsburgh, Kansas,
for five days with a puppy is a story involving
someone else's Datsun and somebody not putting
water in the radiator, and I refuse to assign blame
even in memory, because it was probably me.

My five-year-old believes God works His way
through the alphabet. She doesn't think
A has a lot of power, so it's up to me
to teach her that three of them together
can get you a tow truck, which, a decade
before she was born, led to a garage
whose owner believed that stocking parts
for imports was un-American.

Christmas had just passed and Jesus and
Santa Claus were lit up in almost
everyone's yard. It was a safe place
in the middle of America and people
brought me chicken soup to prove it.
They offered me jobs and called me Honey
and in the made-for-TV movie of my life
I would have married the strong and handsome
mechanic and lived in a Victorian house.

But the mechanic was already married,
and I had a one-story life elsewhere,
temporarily paused. David was still in Illinois,
waiting for that blue Rabbit to resuscitate itself.

I don't know which one of us got the romantic idea
that two broken cars limping across the desert
would be better than one, but for once we didn't argue
and devised a plan to meet in Oklahoma City,
at the house of an old high school friend.
We arrived in the smack center
of his newest dead marriage.

Whatever was lost and sad in the house
kept us up all night laughing, not cruelly,
although it's fair to say not kindly either,
so joyous were we not to be them.
In the early white morning light, how
wonderful it was to leave. And
what a good plan to be ensconced
in separate cars! Everything
seemed like a great idea, especially
those colored light bulbs strung and swinging
in the wind over Main Street intersections.
Even Texas seemed like a good idea.
And how smart of New Mexico not to have changed
their drugstores in thirty years, just so we
could sit at a mahogany soda fountain
sweet on the selves we could have been
in decades past. On the road
we were futuristic in communication
using a code of blinkers and turn signals
to stop ourselves together.

David doesn't remember the gas station attendant,
lacking arms and legs, wheeling himself over to the gas pump
and lifting the pump with his mouth,
though I don't see how he could have missed it.
David does remember a wheelchair
and the man in it calling me "no spring chicken,"
even though I was twenty-seven.
There was a snapshot of a bitterness
which involved a young woman, but we
were just traveling through, not long
enough to get the whole story
unless we were going to make it up ourselves,
which David later did.

Then it got dark and the fog rolled
in like a vertical tumbleweed.
And I thought something with wings hit the car
like an omen. But I couldn't stop.
I had to keep following what was before me.
Those receding, tiny flashing lights
it could be so easy to loose.

Romance

A woman is putting on her shoes.
Then she puts on her face.
It goes like this: eyes, mouth, cheeks.
Against bouquet, both the idea
and its presence (lilac)
she forgets the nose.
Still, in the creation of self,
magnolia can sneak up on you.
Deep Heart, Small Night.

The woman laces up her shoes.

Her bracelet lies on the bed, a circle
of blue stones to rest her head upon.
Such dreams! A man falls
through the mind of the woman
and the consequence to thought
pulls the garter as high
as the imagination can reach.

In the night of blue stones
everyone lies into temporary truth
and the world complies:
the stars are meteoric jewels
the dark of the moon has stopped breathing,
yadda, yadda, yadda.

Tired of metaphor
the woman decides to quit dreaming,
lifts her head, tries for clarity.

The bedroom window
overlooks grass and dangling moss.
Through glass the moss changes its green
from Verdi to Mozart. It's relentless,
the journey from there to here
though there, might be, dear one
here—just one more cliché
farmed out to blue bowls—the kitchen
where the He waits patiently to hear
the drop of the novel upstairs,
the call down the back staircase
from the perpetually dressing She.

Philosophy 101

What appears to be is what is not.
What is not is what appears to be.
The shadow on the Amish Barn
is not a shadow. There are games

some philosophers play while wearing top hats.
Have idea only to deny idea; open and close
the gates of ancient cities
whose pillars have not yet turned to salt.

That's poetry, taking out the extra
ingredient and hoping nobody notices.
In the end, we aren't talking about soufflés,
but the missing air
words go through
and then the missing words themselves.

The simplest landscape
is the most complicated of all,
so the Puritans never reached cactus.
But, like cowboys, they too
had hats and buckles to undo.
Some became Congregationalists,
Works and Acts together in a Pew of Bonnets,
the worship of story manifest:
faith, not such a great leap.

As one of the wise man claims: *a priori*
which is anything you really know—

it's not like the daisy of She loves you
She loves you not—

It's how when you stop
thinking about beauty
beauty comes in, accidentally,
through the hair,

or how when you stop thinking about love
the world stops into silence.
And no amount of math
can reduce nothing.[1]

I am turning it over & over again.
Deflating Pillows. Grainy bed.
What warnings have I missed?
I've been thinking about it.

---

1   Billy Preston

Summer Night

The screen door is dotted
With a necklace of winks
And everyone's porch slip
Is open.

But this is the Midwest
So we have neighborhoods
Of privacy

Where we can close our eyes
Over & over
The body of the other.

The house flickers into the yard
Where iridescent beetles
Chomp grape leaves
Into skeletons.

Nothing is completely simple
Between light & dark.

Saint Lucy gouged out
Her eyes and they reappeared on a platter
Offered to the blind.

On my prayer card they blink
Between wrong and right.

The air smells of rose and citronella,
Of aluminum and rubber.
Sounds: a distant pump organ of crickets
Children being called in
From a different decade.

The streetlights have already come on.

Aging In America

It happens more geographically
than you can imagine:
a Dodge rambling over
a two lane blacktop. Fields:
Goldenrod, Mustard, Cotton, Corn.
Time: Southern. Large.
A winding Kentucky staircase. *Up.*
Children ring rosey round Dogwood,
and the ancestral photos in lavender hallways
have not yet turned sepia.
It is the time where it is impossible
that the old have been young,
which comes right before the time
when it is impossible that the young will be old.
In between, time is exactly as it should be—
Temporal, everlasting summer.
A girl swinging on a tree tire,
someone blowing dandelion seeds
over bottles of Yes.

And then time speeds up.
In Chicago, on Lake Shore Drive,
Teens push pedal to metal.
Headlight streaks curve toward God.
For those who make it around the curve:
shopping: Michigan Avenue.
There are decisions to make over & over,
direction reversals, until, heading west,
everything accelerates again.

On interstates, gas stations are shrines to renewal,
and prayers stream by in a message of litter
as each car exceeds the past, blots it out
like every telephone pole you've passed before.
Tiny cigarette votives brand the land
(ashes, ashes, we all fall down)
but we're already in front of ravage. Front beams
pour out pelts of white radiance into the night.
This is our speed of light, our plural pronoun.
Pilgrims: Our covered wagons are cruising
beyond radar toward

II.

My Elegant Universe

The night I met Tony
        —twenty years ago in Arizona—
I didn't know
        the ways he would pop up

        in the future in books without pictures.
    But then it wasn't unexpected
            that people you didn't know would show up at your door
at midnight and take you someplace you didn't
        know you wanted to go.

This night, people showed up at the married
        student housing Quonset hut
where Phil and I were staying
        not because we were married
but because we were poor,
        and one of us knew the occupant
whose husband had left her and the baby
        with little choice but to become Sheiks
at the Ashram down the street.

It could have been Halloween
        at the door—Ichabod Crane & an elf—
with some blond girl waving from the car,
        but it was summer and I could see right away
they were on a rescue mission and that they were after me.

I don't know how it got around in those
        days before the internet
that things were bad, but certain blocks in Tucson
        were like a village and some idiot went around
spreading bad news until the helicopters showed up
        to shine a light over your house.

I know now that people who appear at
        exactly the right moment can be a trick
but then I was on the couch with the Anatomy &
        Physiology textbook, learning the body.
Phil was already asleep, and I was ready to leave
        every vein behind me.
There was no denying that pretending to be married
        had put us both in a bad mood
like wearing shoes which are too small,
        which the kitchen was.

An hour later we were on Mount Lemmon
        and this is one of the things I love most about memory—
how it doesn't make you recite the car trips
        unless something significant happens, like an accident
or John Braumgartner saying, "this is a two-way street, you know,"
        when "I found love on a two-way street" comes over the radio—
but this much I remember from inside the car:
        on the way up the mountain I saw a woman
walking down. She was see-through
        but she had a sleeping bag, which didn't make any sense
because ghosts shouldn't have to sleep.

        By the time we got out of the car
I knew the blond girl was named Lynn,
        and her boyfriend, Tony.
I was a friend of David who was a friend of Lynn.
        The boyfriend was twice removed
and just a footnote in the expedition for me
        until Lynn and David walked off to go get high
leaving Tony and me to make the best of things,
        and that's when he started interviewing me about love.
It was the question that drove us, in our twenties,
        all over town and through tunnels, sometimes on bicycles.

Still no one asked the question out loud.
    I didn't answer directly but informed him
about the ghost and the sleeping bag
    and the sense that something more animal than us
was on the mountain too
and he told me it wasn't good to state the obvious
which, to be fair, the ghost wasn't.

By the time we got home in the morning
    Phil had already left to build something
but there was coffee and a love note,
    which, when you added in the Shanty at night,
was almost a construction of a life.
And we did some good together:
    when the Ashram woman showed back up at her door
with the baby in her arms, too exhausted from yoga
    to remove the towel from her head,
we fixed her up with a Heber Hotshot
    and they fell in love and moved up North
leaving her hair free to cascade the mountain.

But we got kicked out of being fake married anyway
    and into a teepee, which, as you can imagine,
it was hard to take showers within,
    and after a year, our morning notes were coming
to each other from different states.

I don't know where Phil is now, or David, or Lynn
    but Tony and I knew each other for many years
through continual accident. Once I woke up mid-dream
    on a train in the middle of Texas
to find him lifting a glass of wine mid-air before we derailed
    and once I saw him cutting his toenails
at the back of a poetry reading,
    which few people have the confidence to do.

I know approximately where he lives
        because the back of his books say so
and sometimes I'll see him wandering a conference—
        a ghost of English Departments past.
The coda of what I know about most everyone now
        is written in intellectual graffiti.

I'd been reading Greene's *The Elegant Universe*
        about string theory, and the only way
violins enter in is in reverb subtext.
        Mostly it's the physics of how one atom
pretending to be alone is really connected
        to the other atoms through
an invisible form of time and space,
        but I got stuck in the dark hole of how a woman
can meet a man sixty years too late
        and I don't think there's anything elegant about that.
        So now I'm reading Tony's book
about himself, and, even though it keeps me jumping into the past,
        my daughter doesn't think it's interactive enough.
She brings me the book where the mountains pop out
        of the ground, as we whish the blades
on the windshield of the bus
        whose wheels go round and round.

Restaurants

Before I tried to love someone
out in the open, there was a secret life
built under a tent of camping trips,
in a field, near an Eagles concert.

The band I followed all over the United States
called themselves The Druids
until they rotated bass players
and orbited into The Wooden Planet.

I started to see how one thing
could evolve into something else,
which is what I might have been
practicing for every night

watching the guitar player with an awe
so deep inside me
by the time it arrived at my face,
I ignored him.

In the road days, nutrition involved
talking into a clown's mouth. If spirits
were high, somebody might attempt to
discuss Kant with the clown. Once

a voice from within the clown said
object representation rather than *fuck you.*
The transaction ended with a bag of fries
exiting a tiny window, which proved
the clown's point.

In the rearview window we could see
a world of adult responsibility,
so no one was anxious to disband,
particularly in states
harboring drive-through liquor stores.

By the time we got to Arizona, the sky
had grown so large it was bloated with promise,
and the streaks of sunset pointed in
unlimited direction,
but when the band stopped for breakfast in Tucson,
I stayed at the Pot Belly Cafe
where I met others who appreciated
both the irony of biscuits and gravy
and the biscuits and gravy themselves.

I enlisted in college,
but it was in restaurants
I began to learn the contexts I could
insert content into:

Gentle Ben's was built entirely of logs
and the frat boys lumbered in for
Happy Hour, which they thought
was an actual time.

The Saw Mill Café insisted on the literal
so that you couldn't go anywhere
after you left without leaving a trail of shavings,
and many a person's life was changed
over margaritas at the Crossroads Diner.

The Blue Willow breeze blew
over blue and white plates,
and the jewelry and china
sold at the cash register signified a step
toward something serious. Once my former love
was spotted there with someone else
immediately before he became my former love.

One night, another love and I dressed up,
went out to the Solarium. Glass bubbled
around us. We ordered lobster.
It was my 30th birthday
and one of us thought maybe it was time
to get married, and the other one pulled out
a blue velvet box, which, when opened
didn't reveal a diamond of promise
but a small silver keychain of a zodiac
whose randomness went around in a circle
of animals. He was the fish. I, the ram.

And then I spent many years, in many cities
at tables set with white cloth and candles,
and an enormous bread basket, over which
many different men asked me my sign.
I tried to pay attention, wishing I had
been born under that woman who balanced
the scales on her shoulders,
so nothing would weigh her down.

Tucson, 1982

There was little money then
which made things easier to break into.
Mary said that one night she caught a drunk burglar
trying to carry away her entire house—not the contents
of the house, but the flimsy house itself.

In those days, the whole world
was a doll house we had stepped into
when we left our cities and parents
to waitress at the Crying Onion Café
or bartend at The Borderline Tavern,
in a state where one of the only rules was:
people had to check their guns at the bar.

I was one of those bartenders
who held out her hand to receive
a thirty-eight in exchange for a beer,
my nonchalance, like my suede jacket,
a Western affectation.
Those were the years I tried on everything
to see what would fit,
and except for the cowboy boots
I don't have anything or anybody left.

When men swung through the tavern doors
you'd have to size them up to figure out
which ones might be hiding something besides a wife,
and the concealed sadness they carried.

I don't know which reporter titled the serial rapist
who quoted Hemingway, "Apologetic Rapist,";
titles for the others followed:
"Prime Time", "Bandana", "Pot-bellied".

On the street, the good men
would start whistling something by James Taylor
to proclaim their innocence.
There were reasons I needed to love them,
besides the heartbreak of how awkward
they were in announcing themselves in the world;
a girl needed a steady guy
to walk her to the car.

When the seven-year-old girl snatched from a
Take Back the Night rally was found
murdered in an alley, there was no language
to soften the thing done.
Even searching the underworld of mythology,
it was hard to find a story to make it better.
The Wild West was always romantic fallacy.
Miss Kitty didn't exist.

Still, we tell the tales:
It is almost always
the desert witching hour—
the sky a perpetual purple with infectious
pink streaks. Those two murdered girls
on Lee Street remain in the gloaming,
bound in their rocking chairs like Raggedy Anns,
while Mary and I moved east into a future
of wilder weather, closer to those low wind moans,
that even across country,
sound like La Llorona crying out for lost children.

Good Friday
(Yaqui Reservation, Tucson, Arizona)

These are the faces of Semana Santa mashed
from flour and water into warrior cover.

In the cages the deer dancers jingle
apostolic regret, catholic fear.

Women throw tortillas into air.
The tortillas somersault down: thank you.

A rain washes desert night.
Temporary surprise endures.

All year long the masks have been prepared
for one way of thinking about art.

Tonight under straggling thunder
the Temple will be stormed.

The Birth will be stolen—
a carving whose garment is being.

On Sunday the baby will be returned.
Men will remove their masks & place them in fire.

All those rough drafts will be burned
in anticipation.

The final version of you
is waiting to emerge.

Oracle

It means the place where the revelation
is given, and other things, depending upon
the size of dictionary you're consulting,
but now I'm in Oracle, Arizona and it's not
a round thing or a wise saying
but a place, which is how it happens
in the United States.

They must have thought,
those Wagons of The Previous,
to give comfort, direction in
how the map will play out
but pioneers are historically
rebellious. I'm not the only one
who has cried in What Cheer, Iowa.
or lied in Truth or Consequence, NM
and didn't pay the price until years later.

The real story has Oracle
named after a ship.
I couldn't care less;
I'm here looking for signs
and then there's that big round O
of revelation
that the settlers must have agreed upon—
the irony inherent in names,
like how Gertrude was destined to be beautiful:
a joke that, when true, lasts almost a lifetime
until the turn, like in a sonnet,
when Gertrude grows into herself.

That happened to Route 66.
Nostalgia cruised into the future
via finned automobiles. Look
there's the convertible woman
waving goodbye to gas station dinosaurs.
In Bloomington, Illinois, she crosses
a bridge curving over iron & brick main streets
where the past is buried beside Adlai Stevenson
and then "click" you're in Normal,
a place that doesn't exist as a pun,
but that didn't keep us from running so far
from it that it was the only place we
wanted to end up. And that's the trick;
how things come together
on the internal map
when you least expect it
to be lived in
and with
and named. My love.

Grief
(for Jonson and David)

The gold dog buries her bone
with plans to dig it up again.
The backyard is a graveyard of plot
and forgotten bone and returning to plot.

When Jonson rolled in tar as a puppy,
David and I were happy in comic nuisance:
A dog covered with tar!
Who wouldn't be happy?

Who wouldn't try solvent,
strategic scissoring
before consulting professionals,
before the buzz cut left
her looking like a spotted lamb?

Jonson could shape change:
puppy, dog, lamb, lion.
On top of a mountain
she was statuesque,
and at home
she guarded the door with a wag.
In any scenario with a burglar
I'm not sure I could have let her go first.

She and I were our own fairy tale and cop story.
Once in the woods, I stepped in front
of four German Shepherds
to protect her
and the woods stood still
outside of barking.

There is a way a man's hands
on a dog's stomach
can circle back into memory.

But when Jonson got sick
David couldn't be called back
over phone lines toward
anything toxic and Jonson
had green foam coming out of her
mouth: it was liver or spleen.

When it got so bad
she couldn't take the stairs to pee
I started sleeping outside
with her so I wouldn't
wake up to find her dead

When it got impossible,
I finally called a woman with a syringe.

It was midnight.
The moon was full.
Neighbors came,
but death wasn't pretty
and it didn't relieve anything.

The final thing is never the best
thing you could do
because it's final
and sometimes it's even wrong.

Jonson, it turned out,
didn't want to leave.
Even sick and sedated
she bit at the syringe
but the woman said it was too late.

I went into the house,
waiting for a call of reprieve
And I have never been so unsure
of who has the power to do what
and how do we know
we aren't causing more pain.

Back on the porch
Jonson had vanished but the remains
of a dog were being rolled into a rug.

Years away from an empty house
the phone doesn't ring into,
in the garden near the day lilies,
I keep digging up rotting treasures,
burying them, digging them up again.

Mice

In the children's stories,
they peek out from a hole in a wall.
Such a cozy sight, some of them are knitting.
But my insulation is being carried
from one floor to another,
wires are being gnawed,
and something is living in the silverware drawer.
It is winter and the prairie is giving up its creatures.
In the dark of short days,
tiny movements and dark little shadows
cast warnings about certain things requiring a plan.
I'm not alone in the visitation. Someone says,
"There are two types of people here;
those who have mice and those
who don't know they have mice."
Someone else adds,
"And those who have cats."
In my house it's the dog
who has the final say about cats,
and I'm unwilling to commit
to any kind of carnage,
which is why for months
there was an intricate system
of empty paper towel rolls loaded
with peanut butter, carefully aligned
over a tall plastic can, and when the mice
tipped in, my daughter would name them
and we'd drive them over the highway
into the woods and say good-bye.

They returned with friends.
My mother said, "Who wouldn't
after they heard about
free peanut butter?"
She said this without pride.
Then a neighbor's house burned down,
the result of a mouse chewing through
electrical wire and I got serious—
a little plastic trap house
with a storybook cubbyhole and then
a quick chop of the head
leaving visible only a tiny unwagging tail.
I was like the Queen of Hearts,
but that only worked three times. Finally,
I called an exterminator to deliver blue poison
and I confess, I knew the upcoming
disappearance would be the result of
internal bleeding. Later, there,
in the laundry room, was one,
dead, but curled up
almost like it was sleeping
itself into *Good Night Moon.*

What sorrow I have,
living between books
and the world sometimes.

Praising The Lord

No one knows how
to worship properly
so we settle for heads bowed
in an embarrassment of prayer.
Even when the gospel singers
come in with the Saints,
there's some white guy
afraid to tap his foot.

But this morning I was watching
a substantial woman in the choir
who needed something from the world;
you could tell by the way she was clapping
out of space,
all the air around her was
ripe for slapping
up, down, over, and around.

She was breaking down the rhythm
of what was possible for the congregation
and others were following. A young woman
found something that totally wasn't a beat
to jerk into before she clapped, with exaltation,
into something else that wasn't a beat,
a spiritual portal no one else could enter in time.

I think the Holy Spirit didn't major in music,
or aesthetics, and that all the beatific paintings
of women glowing up in spiritual ecstasy
are post-coital, and the Thing Itself
isn't pretty or synchronized,
but squeaky and annoying
like a rogue grocery cart wheel
rolling you down some unexpected aisle
filled with tuna and sacred candles
toward the checkout.

God is the cashier, of course,
and how you know it's Her
is that the line is long with the maimed
containing their peas in jail-cell carts,
and some of the damaged have been
in jail themselves,
or a least a sorority. And yet,
in front of the tabloids and cigarettes,
you suddenly know that everyone
is so damned loved
that you silently tell the old man
with hair coming out of his ears
and the girl with prolific acne
that you love them too. And
the little boy running toward the candy
hears you and claps.

Healing

It came one day
Simple as a cornfield
Sprung from summer
Burned into ground

We didn't believe It
Could go anywhere else
Someone chose It for us
Said this time It's yours

It was simple
Until It wasn't
It was the way
The red hawk

Flew beyond madness
Into the trees
The way we looked
Toward the sun

As if It belonged.

III.

The Call

This is the night I already know
That when I sleep, all the dream birds
Will dip into a pattern of regret.

This is the night I will
Want to call you
And the desert will attempt
To heal me from *Want,*
The night of javelina eyes,
Blind & blazing.

It's as simple as dumped garbage:
God working through animals
To reveal a mess all my own.

Coyotes trick wind
Toward mission bells.
Listen: they ring
And ring and ring into air.

The End of the World Weather

At the end of the world
the weather in the Midwest is surprisingly breezy.
It's November. The leaves have started
falling and then stopped.
At a time when branches are usually bare
some trees remain green and tall
against a sky Magritte might have painted.

The day has turned early into dark
but people are still sitting outside
on porch swings and picnic tables,
watching the world lumber on.

Halloween was two weeks ago.
On that night, a torrential rain fell.
Only the undecorated teenagers lumbered
about the streets, black garbage bags
held above their heads, while
small fairies and witches
stayed inside handing out candy
to the ordinary,
which is something like how the weather
has been reversed.

Beside my porch, in the hackberry tree,
birds have paused in their journey south.

All across the country
the weather has been putting people
in their places or taking them out
and setting them down someplace else.
Or, things have been just been misplaced.
Even smells. One step that doesn't break
mother's back, there's a crisp leaf aroma,
the next step: *lavender, hibiscus.*
Who knows what it all means?
But there are other things going on
suggesting the climate doesn't bode well.

Hurricane lamps dot my porch
and from the lawn chair,
I watch as the bicyclists
whip through already fallen gold.
Little leaf funnels rise up
toward wayward chirping.
I am thinking: *Berries, Magritte,*
Apple Pie.
And how hard it would be to give it all up
in a flash, or through slow suffocation,
because even in this,
it's lovely the way we destroy ourselves.

Mosaic

Things are breaking. Things are breaking.
Two storm doors. One tile plate.
One window pane. One mason jar.
Multiple crystal wine glasses.
Who is to blame?
The teenagers who pound too hard on doors,
slam them shut hard to make sure
you know they'll be back?
Myself, neglector of bringing pots in off the porch,
me, who believes my name alone
makes me a worthy opponent of wind?
Or the named storm, breaker
of trees and roofs? I do tip my hat
in that direction before it blows away.
Even the soft things aren't safe.
The dog has chewed the couch
and it is broken in a very muted way.

My mother too is breaking down
her persona, as she forgets
the world, fragment by fragment.

How to mend all the damage?
Glue isn't as invisible as it thinks.
I've been wrong about so many things,
but Stanford, they may have found
a cell responsible for breaking plaque
in the frontal lobe and mice are playing
with a cure that won't get here in time.
Meanwhile, we can still break bread,
exchange viewpoints.

Here are memories
shed for you, daughter:
The fife terriers running on the farm.
The Duncan Phyfe table.
The cold nights in Scotland.

I will take them on, mother
Remember the blood soup?
All the culinary adventures
until you got to haggis and stopped?

I was a girl who could break-dance,
a woman who had her heart broken,
and I know nothing is worse than being afraid.
Go ahead: throw the pots and pans into air
without worry of vases on the sill;
let's puzzle out the jagged beauty
emerging from shards of blue glass.

We are beyond making things whole,
but we are not beyond making stories.
There is a small girl
in a turquoise Nash Rambler
and her mother is wearing a pink dress
and the girls' cheek is against her mother's dress
forever.

Dreaming Myself Awake

The living sleep
so that the dead can live.
Last night everybody
crowded and rushed
to catch the midnight train
to the world where
the dead wait.

The ride was a veined subway
of architecture, each platformed pause
designed around a portion of body—
hands harnessed, eyes envied green
kidneys lacking the shape of pools.
At the final stop somebody's imagination
hadn't been able to extricate the baseball diamond
so the dead stood in center field.

Without beach houses to distract,
the dead were more themselves than ever,
an absence of personality so severe that
invisible idiosyncrasies walked around
sporting canes and eye patches.

The dead were not necessarily wise,
or even, classically, there,
and still we defined ourselves
by calling out to them.
When they answered, we didn't
understand their accent.

Lacking language and body
the mind creates elevators and oceans.
When I dreamed myself awake
I was surfing against currents,
and when I opened my eyes
I had neglected to ask
what would be required of me
to give up anything.
I hadn't forgotten the feel
of cotton or the belief
that gravity could hold me
in the morning of your arms.
I did not return to sleep
but stood tentative guard
to welcome you back
from all the tunnels you traveled
all the seas you neglected to drown

I Did Very Little Today

Somewhere in my century,
people are out fighting Ebola
or creating other germs to destroy us,
a whole global chess match,
and I wonder what drives everybody
to churn forward constructing and erasing
buildings and highways. It's so impressive
and yet I did very little today. I made no butter.
I went to my healer, who placed anointed hands
over my heart and brought me into the present.
"It burns," she says, "with grief," and I say I'm over that.
I don't have time for it anymore. I have a lot of laundry.
Still, my days of doing very little have added up,
and people younger than me are getting sick.
"I don't have the work ethic for cancer," I tell the healer
and she says she knows, which is why it's good
to yank out all the grief and icebergs before they turn into tumors.
"There's an iceberg?" I'm coy.
I know where it is. Left breast. But it's hot. Hot ice.
"You gave up the ring," the healer says, and I know full well
who I didn't marry, but I make her tell me anyway
that it's been him chasing me for decades in my dreams.
"He's more tortured," she says and I know
because I've seen the pictures, but he is very busy
and has many houses and only one wife who isn't me,
and I have some cards falling down and no husband who isn't him.
The healer moves her hands to my feet, which begin to prickle.
"I'm trying to put you back on the ground."
Afterwards, I was tired, but grounded.
I felt sad about a comedian who had committed suicide
but that didn't seem like an excuse for not doing anything.
I took to the Bible to relieve sadness, but different verses do
different things and good cheer isn't inevitable.

I think about Martha and Mary (not the Virgin)
and how no one ever accused me of being Martha.
Someone over a neighborhood listserv asks
if they can hire someone to do their ironing. Ironing!
Starch is still a part of a lot of people's lives.
It has been a very long time since I have ironed.
The healer and I had talked about aging
and creating a cosmetic that can turn back time,
but I know I won't be the one to create it,
not because of the chemistry, but the physics.
My grandfather—he pops in all the time even though he's dead—
said he always thought there would be nothing to do in old age
but when he got old, chores took a lot longer.
He did a lot. Farmed and built and shouldered things
and lifted garage doors to reveal a Cadillac.
He makes me feel bad about not farming anything,
but I console myself with the basil. I've done very little today.
I fixed no machines. I made no bread. I went to Strawberry Fields
and bought an energy shake and talked with the cashier
about how the healer informed me that one of my coworkers
had inserted daggers into my solar plexus.
"Oh," said the cashier, "when she worked here she just stole."
Some people get all the luck and I'm not one of them.
Now a day in which I have done very little has passed
but not really because of that late summer light trick,
where the sky is moving westward into turquoise.
It's time to take the dog for a walk and meet a friend
for pinot grigio, but before I get there the landscape changes
into that color that is so lovely no one can describe it
but here:
The illuminated trees are considering a turn toward threat,
but, for a moment, the incontrovertible sky retains power,
and oaks, maples, redbuds mute into transcendent still life.
Someone should grab an easel or say something.
I wish I could, but the sky . . . and the trees . . .
Who in the world (thank you all)
would want to do anything that would miss it?

Where The Time Goes

In middle age you have to start tracking money and time
to see what world they are disappearing into.
There's coffee of course and that speeds things up.
The coffee pot has made it all the way from the fifties
to my kitchen, its golden spheres portending
a glamorous hat and a good time in space.
Speaking of objects, there is a tiny pincushion chair on the piano
that would look better in Nicole's dollhouse
and that requires a post office,
which is almost an antiquated idea come to life, decorated
with bars and cubicles and tiny iron combination locks.
I wish there were a letter for me.
I know what decade I want it to be from, but there's a mailbox
in the 1990s I'm afraid is always going to be empty.
After errands, I call my father, and we speak of the daily obituaries,
which we always do, and today we talk about how
either Click or Clack can make us laugh, even in death.
I think of my 1974 Dodge Dart, and how the slant-six engine
was spoken of with the reverence certain objects deserve,
and I don't think that's idolatry.
I ask about my mother, who is stubbornly fading away,
and whether she can still vote and my father says by mail.
But he and I, we are waiting out the rain;
we love the polling places with the little curtains
where we can blacken circles and emerge like the Wizard of Oz,
who did, after all, have some power once he got over himself.
After voting, I talk to friends in the message part of Facebook
about how my dead ex-boyfriend appeared to me
on the computer screen and seemed to open his eyes,
and no one questions it because
he appears on their screens too and as one person said,
"Photoshop can do a lot with eyes."

I don't report that, when his eyes opened up,
I told him, "You would not believe where you are right now,"
because, well, he would. Outside it is nearing Holidays,
and my mother's attic is filled with porcelain bakeries
and steepled churches and train stations.
I wonder if I brought them down and arranged
the pretend town around her she would feel part
of a world again. That's what love has become
—creating buildings with tiny lights inside—
but here, it is happening again: my mind is taking me away
from fiscal duty back into the village of consideration,
and when I am this far gone, all I can do is pray myself back.
Please God, don't let me enter any attics or basements;
protect me from the refrigerator, from all the animals needing petting,
from the part of myself that can fly away toward imaginary towns.
Protect me from telephones, hair salons, and fallen leaves;
lead me down the path of the organized, the can-do people,
the fruitful. Let me dwell in the moment, at the desk
of works, of forms, of things potentially said and done.

Elegy for Louisette

We live in a house, on a street, in a town,
in a state, in a country, and I could go on and on
with this trope, but it makes me lonely—
expanding out into a Universe where someone
was cruel enough to strap a dog into space.
I will return to my block where the outlines of sky blue
were chalked into memory a generation before me,
where Betty Ann is always telling me
about the ghost of a grocery store down on Race Street
and the butcher who telephoned the neighborhood
informing housewives they were having pot roast tonight
because someone had killed a cow.
Three blocks away the Ross's named their daughter Betsy,
which made her think she had to fly an American flag
every day of her life. We could be fooled into thinking
we lived decades in back of brick streets and globe lights,
but we keep circling the block past the Lincoln statue,
past the century-old arboretum into the Present,
which is titled by everybody's Wi-Fi handle:
Wrigley, Lucky, Spazoid—whatever we wish for, or fear.

And now, I want to speak of Louisette and her tulips.
The primary colors came to her yard first. Her garden trick:
move outside the lines into controlled wildness.
Bloom to weed, and then the trick of weed bloom.
Her explanation for no grass:
"One day I decided to tear it all up and start anew,"
and then anew began the progression:
snowbells to tulips to milkweed, yarrow, morning glory, forget-me-nots.

The bells to the Northwest are Catholic and academic,
but still they ring for thee and thee and then, me too.
In the meantime, there are lit stars on porches
guiding people home
to practice the neighborly etiquette of jam
and not hearing too much. The elders continue
the necessary work of retelling the story
of the boulevard that no longer exists
because if we don't teach these things
they go underground. Not all advice is spoken:
Dig it up, start anew, there are perennials
that will return from memory
and weeds that will surprise you with their beauty.

Curtain Call

Floating beyond the light of the city, in the glory
of desert, coyotes were howling an unapproved rendition
of *America The Beautiful*. Everything was a story.

In the details of Santa Ana winds there was a worry
permeating creosote, sending post-it notes of perdition
floating beyond the city lights into the quarry.

They said odd things, these notes: He was sorry;
the scene had gone wrong in the kitchen
of America, where everything was a story.

In the kitchen, the domestic was almost starry:
teapot, radio, clock. The tarot magician
floated beyond the lights of city, beyond glory.

The characters were changeable—the women, an inventory
of love and maroon; men who dressed in tuxedoed fiction.
In America the Beautiful, everything was a story.

And then, in a quiet quarry, the curtain floated
up and down. The lights of the city flicked off.
In America, the story was the glory.
The story was everything. Everything was the story.

Porch Swing

There is a lake then   rising   from late evening
Water   for the mind

& in this lake, a discussion among fish.

        Me   I have become
   this patience   porch & swing inherited
   deep down
       in imagination   a canoe to
turn over & over again   in my sleep.

The fish   surface   to ponder Neitzsche.
      It's only bait:
I want body   I want
      Catch
the deep continual row   across the lake toward another

narrative   where it's early desert
     where light bobs
to the surface
      of creosote   where
the child   and I   and the man

live just above the surface
of each other
     where
the cradle of desire rocks the unborn

& the woman (I)
      (remember I)
awakens to search cupboards
      slight prescient smell (Watermelon/Musk)

I can hardly wait to return.

Acknowledgments

Thanks to the following publications where these poems were originally published.

Postcard, *Tamaque*
Dead Poets House, The Call, *Rhino*
Road Trip, *The Wisconsin Review*
Autobiography, *Museum of Americana*
Romance, Fishing, Oracle, *Another Chicago Magazine*
Good Friday, *Women Made Gallery*
Restaurants, *New Mexico Poetry Review*
Dreaming Myself Awake, *Boulevard*
Philosophy 101, Aging In America, My Elegant Universe, *Spoon River Poetry Review*
The End of the World Weather, *Exquisite Corpse*

Acknowledgement is also given to Jason Berg for the story that led to the poem "Praising the Lord."

Thanks to The Virginia Center For The Creative Arts and The Ragdale Foundation for such wonderful space and time and new friendships.

Thanks to the Glass Room Poets (Robert Manchester, Julie Price, Elizabeth Majerus, John Palen, & Matthew Murray) for Sunday afternoon revision, to Pam Gemin, John Crawford, Merle Turchik, and Todd Lieber for considerations and friendship, and to Donald Eugene Walden for consistent, lifelong support.

photo: Claire Renee Billingsley

Gale Renee Walden is the author of the poetry book *Same Blue Chevy* (Tia Chucha/Northwestern University Press). Her fiction and non-fiction have appeared nationally in literary and mainstream magazines. Her work has won the Boston Review Annual Fiction Prize and was noted as distinguished in the 2006 *Best American Short Stories*. She has been a feature poet in *The Spoon River Poetry Review*. She considers ordinary time and landscapes of Americana, traveling from desert to prairie, childhood to aging and back again, in this, her newest collection, *Where The Time Goes*.

CPSIA information can be obtained
at www.ICGtesting.com
Printed in the USA
LVOW03s2020290317
528973LV00001B/10/P